'No Longer Dead to Me'

Working with schoolchildren in the performing and creative arts

*Edited by Sally Woodhead
and Adrian Tinniswood*

The National Trust

Preface

No Longer Dead to Me explores and celebrates some of the more innovative ways in which the performing and creative arts are playing their part in the education of our children. It seems fitting that this process should be taking place under the auspices of the National Trust, an organisation that has devoted more than a century to saving and protecting other, more tangible expressions of our cultural heritage. There is no better way for schoolchildren to understand and appreciate that heritage than through the medium of the arts.

Too often in recent years, the contribution that the performing arts have made to education has been undervalued. Theatre-in-Education companies have closed down; funding has been progressively cut back; and as the millennium approaches, the movement as a whole stands in danger of withering away through a lack of financial support. Whatever else the essays in *No Longer Dead to Me* tell us – and they tell us a great deal – one message comes through loud and clear. The opportunities for learning and enjoyment offered by the arts are too exciting, the potential rewards too great, for us to allow them to be lost.

SIR ANTHONY HOPKINS

Foreword

Since human society began, the arts have been the means by which we have chosen to communicate our highest values and noblest instincts. *No Longer Dead to Me* demonstrates this to be as true today as it has ever been. For children to gain fresh perceptions of the past through drama, or to develop an enhanced appreciation of landscape through painting and sculpture, is important. But it is the *activity*, the artistic process itself, which is truly important. It liberates the creativity in every child.

William Morris, whose deep concern for our heritage did so much to pave the way for the founding of the National Trust, once spoke of a 'time when all men would be artists, and the audience for the arts would be nothing less than the whole people'. The evidence of this book suggests that in one sense, at least, Morris was right. With guidance and encouragement, all children *can* be artists. They are the richer for the experience, and so are we.

SIR DAVID PUTTNAM

SALLY WOODHEAD AND ADRIAN TINNISWOOD

Making things with your heart

Sally Woodhead and Adrian Tinniswood discuss the National Trust's contribution to learning through the arts.

For nearly two decades the National Trust has been committed to education through the arts

*I*t is the 1890s, and in the rich mahogany splendour of the Library at Lanhydrock in Cornwall, Pre-Raphaelite beauties stare down on a gathering of workers, servants, philanthropists and industrial magnates. Centre stage is Mr Dinsdale, a self-made factory owner.

This is Dinsdale's moment of triumph. In the course of a heated debate over the future of a neighbouring common, he and his fellows have stunned their opponents into silence with the brilliance of their arguments. Nothing now stands in the way of his scheme to create a quarry on the common.

But at the back of the Library a servant girl rises to her feet. She opens her mouth to speak, but no words come. You can see that her workmates are silently willing her to say something, but she seems overcome with embarrassment, and moves as if to sit down again. Then, with a tremendous effort, she points her finger straight at Dinsdale and cries, 'I know he has promised us all work, and money in his quarry. He wants you to think that he's nice. He says he's making

us jobs – but he isn't making them with his heart!' Now it is the turn of the industrialists to be struck dumb, and the debate is rekindled with fresh vigour as the others in the room are carried along by the power of the servant's words.

If you have been lucky enough to encounter a situation like this – a Young National Trust Theatre performance that took place at Lanhydrock a few years ago – you will be familiar with the empowering potential of drama in an educational context. The 'servant girl' was actually a nine-year-old primary school pupil who, through this experience, had somehow bridged the gap between the 1990s and the world of the late 19th century. Of course, children do not need to be actually inside a Victorian country house in order to enter into a roleplay about conservation in Victorian times: drama is a powerful and effective teaching tool, whatever the surroundings. However, it cannot be denied that an historic site provides a particular creative stimulus. It is the particularity of that experience, the unique quality of that stimulus, that we seek to describe and capture in *No Longer Dead to Me*.

Participatory drama

For almost two decades now, the National Trust has had a commitment to education through the performing and creative arts at its properties. The charity's first major venture in the field was the founding of the Young National Trust Theatre in 1977. Up to this point, a visit to an historic site had generally been restricted to observation. There was an occasional piano recital in the Great Hall, or an open-air performance of *A Midsummer Night's Dream* in the gardens, perhaps; but these were passive and predominantly adult-oriented pastimes. With the arrival of the Young National Trust Theatre, country houses and their surroundings would be used in a exciting new way, as the performing

arts were brought into play to open the Trust's doors to thousands of young people.

The first director of the YNTT was Dot McCree; she and her small company put together an initial production at Sudbury Hall in Derbyshire, with the support of the then-custodian, John Hodgson, whose lifelong commitment to learning through the arts has been a driving force behind the movement. The idea was to involve schoolchildren in a piece of historical Theatre-in-Education, part script and part improvisation. Several weeks were spent in researching the story of the 17th-century Hall from its beginnings up to the present day, and a production was devised which was intended to reconstruct life in the house during its heyday.

The venture was a success, and the formula was subsequently repeated at other National Trust houses. Queen Elizabeth I visited Knole in Kent, for example, and a Victorian Christmas was held at Lanhydrock. The productions were all participatory; at every point the children who came along were encouraged to interact directly with the characters played by the actors. Music, dance and costume were key elements. However, due to the amount of research needed

for each project, only a few sites could be visited each season, and it soon became clear that the YNTT was unable to meet the growing demand from schools for its work. The answer was to devise a piece that was not site-specific, a generic story that could easily transfer to different properties while still being linked to a specific period.

As a result, the focus switched to an investigation of major historical events – the Civil War, life in Britain during the Second World War, Popish plots and anti-Catholicism during the reign of Charles II, the impact of the French Revolution on the English aristocracy. With this new emphasis came the development of an artistic policy that is just as crucial today as it was when it was formulated in the 1980s:

■ all dramatic work should give the participating child an opportunity to deepen his or her understanding of history and cultural heritage in the context of an historic site

■ the child should always encounter a rich blend of the performing arts

■ the creative experience should give the child access to a heritage which is theirs to enjoy.

The YNTT at Sutton House, Hackney, in 1994 – the creative experience should give a child access to a heritage which is theirs to enjoy

A creative response to the environment

A child muses on the fate of a French aristocrat in the YNTT's 1989 show, REVOLUTION!

Over the years, as external funding has come in from various sources – Lloyds Bank, Barclays Bank and, most recently, S.C. Johnson Wax – the company has increased its size to the current level of six professional actors, and extended its annual tour to around nine venues (rising to fifteen in 1995, when the Theatre put on a special show to celebrate the National Trust's Centenary). The YNTT is now able to call upon a pool of experienced actor-teachers, writers, directors, musicians, designers and educationalists, all of whom regularly make a valued contribution to the creative process.

Just as importantly, strong links have been built with individual teachers across England, Wales and Northern Ireland. The YNTT now tours from May to October every year, and in the course of its work it reaches over 8,000 schoolchildren – mainly at Key Stages 2 and 3, although the company also works with older students when the opportunity presents itself. This partnership with schools and other educational institutions is crucially important, for a performance is most successful when the participants have been well prepared in the classroom beforehand. Prior to each production, resource materials are distributed and briefing courses held to help the teacher. The YNTT also strives to make its work of practical use by choosing to dramatise historical issues which feature in National Curriculum History.

Generous support over the last few years has given the company an opportunity to make new departures. In 1990 a 'Beach Show' toured resorts in Dorset and Devon, taking a sideways look at the serious issue of coastal pollution. And particularly innovative are the Performing Arts in Trust residencies, which use selected National Trust sites as an inspirational focus, enabling young people to express their feelings of place and history through drama, movement, music and storytelling.

Culture and the curriculum

As with any artistic enterprise, it is important that creative projects in the National Trust move forward. In recent years, the Trust's programme of learning through the arts has expanded to include locally-based living history sessions at many of its properties. There is also a number of drama workshops in different parts of the country. The 'War Child' programme, for example, which takes place at several country houses in Derbyshire, explores what it was like to be an evacuee during the Second World War. And, of course, there is the separate but related subject of how artists in residence can inspire creative responses to National Trust properties in children. This is an important part of the Trust's educational work; as a case study, the partnership between artists, schools and the Trust in Cornwall is described in detail by Roger Butts on pages 12-15.

The Young National Trust Theatre has also moved forward. In a departure from its original brief to work on dramatic reconstructions of life in the past, the company now tends to focus on issues. This approach means that the minutiae of daily life, while obviously still important to the success of the show, take second place to an exploration of complex and demanding social and political questions that are still relevant today – religious persecution in the reign of Mary Tudor, for example (*An Endless Maze*, 1992), or monarchism and the Commonwealth (*The Tree Grows Still*, 1994). For the future, the YNTT has plans to create new forms of theatre using the natural environment, to run history-through-drama workshops for adults and to offer developmental courses for teachers on the use of creative and performing arts at historic sites.

There are many references in this book to memorable moments of child participation, and even more that have had to be omitted for want of space. But one incident not mentioned by other contributors is too good to leave out. At Sutton House in Hackney, which is now the home of the YNTT, the local school had just enjoyed taking part in the dress rehearsal for *Virtues and Vanities*, a recent production set in the 1680s. They had all been caught up in political intrigues around the central issue, which concerned the arranged marriage of one of the central characters, Mistress Phillida, to a merchant named Scattergood. It soon became clear that some had been more involved than others. The next morning a member of staff was called to the front door to meet a small boy, who clearly should have been at school. He demanded to see Phillida and Scattergood, and was quite distraught to learn that they weren't there. Only a promise that a message would be relayed to the couple could induce him to leave.

Clearly that particular moment in the past was no longer dead to him. ∎

Arts in Trust in action at Dyrham Park, near Bath

THE NATIONAL TRUST

In January 1895, a small group of conservationists and reformers, led by Octavia Hill, Robert Hunter and Hardwicke Rawnsley, founded a private charity dedicated to acquiring and protecting beautiful and historic countryside, coastline and buildings.

The National Trust for Places of Historic Interest or Natural Beauty, as the new organisation was called, differed from other similar groups in that from the first it aimed to be not so much a pressure group, agitating for legislative change, as a holding body, actually owning and guarding those parts of our national heritage which might otherwise be destroyed.

Today the National Trust – still a charity – is the country's largest private landowner, caring for historic houses and castles, over 243,000 hectares of coast and countryside, ancient monuments, farms and villages.

To catch the conscience

The play's the thing, says John Fines. But what do we mean by 'play'?

'Just run away and play.' 'We were only playing.' 'Stop playing about.' 'Stop work now and go out to play.'

How many uses are there for the word 'play' that suggest it is unimportant, silly, something we should grow out of? Yet when we look at young children learning the most difficult things they will ever learn in their whole lives – speaking a language fluently, learning behaviours for a whole culture, coping with a world full of dangers – how do they do it? They learn through play, the fastest, most efficient, most effective learning medium of all. We receive children into formal schooling when they are already highly skilled and experienced in this form of learning. And what do we do? We try to wean them off it, offering much poorer media in its place.

Thirty years ago, when I was already an experienced teacher of history, I went to a lecture by a lady called Dorothy Heathcote. I had a PhD in History and knew a great deal; she had left school with no qualifications and worked in a mill before going to drama school. She rocked me on my heels, and I went to watch her teach.

This was the second lesson of a sequence, revolving around an illuminated manuscript the children had made in the previous month. There were sixty in the group and the drama was to fill something like seven whole mornings, with the children following the manuscript through time from its writing in Northumbria to today. In the first lesson, Mrs Heathcote had worked with two groups. One, the smaller, were monks. The other consisted of local peasantry.

As she started the second lesson she asked the monks whether they could just get on. Airily, they said yes, they could; and she turned to the peasants. 'I'm right fed up with all this rain,' she said. 'Are you?' One little girl volunteered that it hadn't stopped in three weeks. She asked then what effect it was having on the seedcorn for next year. They quickly told her that it had all rotted. She inquired, with a light in her eye, whether the monks would have any, and a

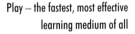
Play – the fastest, most effective learning medium of all

breathless child told her, 'Aye, they've got a dry barn full – and I saw one of them putting a new lock on the door yesterday.'

The lesson continued, and for me, the experienced history teacher, it was the shock of a lifetime. To spend *all this time* on one subject! To teach such large numbers at once! To ask children just to get on, with confidence such that they did! To set up situations that seemed designed to instigate a riot! To get children talking so quickly, and to listen to them with such apparent concern! It went against everything I knew and could do. All the children I had taught so far had been on the outside, looking on while I gave fevered descriptions of what I saw. These children were on the inside, and from that day forward I determined to transform my teaching, to get for my children at least something of what Dorothy so regularly and with such apparent ease got for hers.

Make-believe

One of the thoughts that has borne me up through the years is the simple nostrum that if you really *believe* you are Napoleon, the men in white coats should be sent for at once. The word 'belief' is in itself dangerous and we should be aware of how to take on a role effectively before ever entering the scene.

Watch children playing 'doctors and nurses' (not for too long, or you will see too much and feel that you ought to do something about it). The children don't believe they *are* doctors and nurses. They know that it is going to be fun taking on these roles, and although the rules are hard to keep, the longer you can keep them the more fun it will be. They know that they will learn something, that if you hang on in there as a doctor you will start to know the world from a new angle. You can practise things that are not allowed or even possible in the real world.

A week ago I had my young great-nephews staying with me. They preferred play-cooking to the real thing. With real cooking I had to keep saying, 'No! That's hot, hot, hot!' With play-cooking they could wrap a jumper round a bowl and carry 'hot, hot, hot' carefully without spilling a drop. But if you had come along and stopped our game and said, 'Is there really anything in your bowl, Nathan?', or 'Did you really almost spill the cake-mix, Michael?', they would have looked at you as if you were an idiot. And they would have been right.

When we enter a drama, we accept that there is an interesting problem to explore, that this is a good and pleasing way of exploring that problem. For the time being we accept the rules of the game – because we want to find out.

OK so far. But for many historians there is a difficulty. What about authenticity? What about getting it right? Can you let children replay the Battle of Waterloo and allow them to make Napoleon win? Isn't that dangerous? Won't they end up with the wrong end of the stick?

The YNTT on the Home Front in 1987 – when we enter a drama, we accept the rules of the game because we want to find out more

First, let us deal with the notion of 'danger'. What if children *do* grow up thinking that Napoleon won at Waterloo? Setting aside the millions of Frenchmen who secretly feel that way, I can't imagine a single circumstance in which this strange delusion could hurt someone. Accurate historical information is only needed by people enquiring into the subject to which it relates – historians, and children when they are studying history. They don't need it for all time.

Furthermore, when you look at what historians really do, it is painfully close to what drama does. Some years ago a group of American academics tried to assess the significance for American history of major factors like the railway and slavery, by taking them away from the record and postulating what might have happened without them. A lot of historians shouted; but many showed interest, because that is the kind of thing historians really do. They say, 'What if?' and 'How come?' and 'Maybe we got it wrong – let's put it another way and see how it looks.' We are all revisionists.

Marital difficulties

But that's for clever historians, you may say. Surely kids can't do that? Over recent years there has been a big push to say that empathy is an impossible goal for young children, that the history they can do must be different from the history that adults do. Of course. Who would be foolish enough to believe anyone can think themselves absolutely into the past? Who would say that young children of average ability can read or calculate as well as adults? What they are doing is starting, beginning the process, taking on the tasks at their own level. Naturally their achievements will be at a lower level than those of history professors, but what they must be doing is still history.

Is empathy an impossible goal for children?

Essentially, drama looks for a problem to explore. It doesn't seek to tell a story. Of course there always needs to be a story to provide the context for the problem, but it is not the plot that matters. *Hamlet* is not too good as a story – but Hamlet's problem obsesses us still.

Let me try to illuminate what I mean with a recent example. I had been asked to work with a class of six-year-olds who had been doing a little on Henry VIII. They knew he was fat, irascible, had many wives and was a king. That was their 'story'. So I began to explore it with them by asking whether it was nice to be a king, and they could give me plenty of reasons why it was nice.

They felt confident now, so I was able to put a more difficult problem. Did kings and queens ever have problems? They thought hard and volunteered some examples – wearing a heavy crown, for example. After a while I suggested

that Henry VIII had a problem, and asked whether they would like to meet him. They wanted to very much; but I said this was hard, what with him being dead. But I was good at pretending – could they cope? Could they cope with the formality of court, with a dangerously angry man? They considered it carefully and said they would try.

So we all knew what we were doing, and when I went to a chair at the opposite side of the room, they were ready to come to court and bow or curtsey, as appropriate. I told them my difficulties with Catherine of Aragon, and at once they offered advice. 'Kill her', said a sweet little girl at the front. I expressed terrible shock; I still liked Catherine, and surely it would be wrong – and terribly bad publicity – to kill her? No, they said. You're the King, you can do what you like.

So we went to 'Catherine' to talk it over with her. Quickly the children spilled the beans about Henry's new girlfriend, even though the boys (cowards to a man) were worried about getting their heads chopped off. They were impressed by Catherine, and saw that she had a case. It wasn't proving so easy.

We had been working for an hour, so we had a break, and then came back to seek out Anne Boleyn (still yours truly, by the way – no funny hats, no props, just the agreement that I would try to *be* her if they would try to *see* her). Like Henry, they fell head over heels for her. She was young, flighty, keen on dancing and longing to be queen. The children deserted Catherine's cause at once, but still said there would be problems.

Finally, nearly two hours in, they came back to meet the King and offer their advice. A number were for a quick divorce, while a significant group favoured changing the law so that I could have two wives. ('You can, you know. You're the King'.) A final small group – two boys in fact – marched up hand in hand to say bravely, 'You'll have to wait. When Catherine is dead you can take the ring off her finger and put it on your girlfriend's, and then she will be your wife.' I exploded with rage, but the boys stood their ground, growing in righteousness as they did so.

What was I playing at? Well, I was using a little bit – a very little bit – of historical information. I was using the children's capacity to play. I was using their knowledge about marital breakdown

(and like most classes of any age, they clearly knew a lot). I provided a situation in which we could use all this knowledge in order that we might do some historical thinking – but we were also concerned just as much with today.

We were using the play to catch the conscience of the King, but also to help us think about problems of conscience in general. I have already indicated that historical knowledge *per se* is not of the slightest use. It is when we apply it that it becomes valuable. Historians apply it to refine their understanding of the past, but historians are few and far between, and frankly we don't need too many of them. We ordinary folk happily apply historical knowledge to understand ourselves a little more, to understand the complexity of the situations people have to face, to see the depths of villainy and the heights of sainthood some people can achieve and, above all, to learn to respect diversity – the fact that in different times and different circumstances and different places people may respond in ways that at first strike us as strange – just because they *are* different.

As an adviser to the Young National Trust Theatre over the past few years, I have been privileged to watch as actors utilised the potential of historic sites to enable children to enter the past, and to use their talent for play to learn more about the world. I have seen children struggling to make sense of a 17th-century madwoman who might hold the secret of life and the key to the future. I have seen them in the 16th century, having lived through the restoration of Roman Catholicism under Mary Tudor, facing up to the future with a Protestant Queen Elizabeth. Most recently, I have seen them in late Victorian Britain, vigorously arguing against Octavia Hill's struggle to found the National Trust. Each time we found ourselves for some moments swept away into a new reality when the play no longer mattered, where there were no distinctions between children and actors. They were 'allowed' to become real – a thing we so rarely do with children, because of our fear of what might happen.

What *does* happen is that we go home with our spirits heightened, our eyes opened, our imaginations turned and our consciences stirred. That is what I call real education. ■

Discussing the future of the Commonwealth at Petworth House, West Sussex – it is only when we apply historical knowledge that it becomes valuable

ROGER BUTTS

Arts in Trust

Roger Butts describes some successful partnerships between schools and creative artists.

I recently spent a week living with groups of children as a Romano-Briton at Chysauster, an ancient village near Penzance. In costume, the children worked around one of the huts there, performing tasks which the people of that time must also have carried out – tasks to do with cooking and eating, keeping warm and dry, and coping with everyday problems. We know, though, that life in those days was not just about the necessities. We know that representation and decoration – art – were also of enormous importance to those people. Rooted deep within them was the need to sing, to dance, to draw and paint.

Some time before undertaking our project, I attended a lecture by Nick Johnson, the Director of the Cornwall Archaeology Unit. Nick made a comment that set me thinking: 'Don't imagine that people two or three thousand years ago were any different in essence from yourselves. Don't think that their basic requirements were any different from your own.' This works both ways. In using what we know of our own needs to try to understand people in the past, we should perhaps try harder to use what we know of the past to understand ourselves. If we do, we will come to realise that

Poet Bob Devereux working with children at Antony House, Cornwall

Sculpture by Key Stage 1 pupils – deep within us all is the need to express ourselves in dance, music and art

the arts in their various forms are just as important to us as they were to our long-ago ancestors. Deep within us is the need to express ourselves in dance, music and art. That need is a natural part of our being, and we have to resist the tendency to consign the arts to the back of the educational cupboard, to consider only technological subjects as being worthy of real attention.

Those who call for a return to more traditional methods of teaching – more chalk-and-talk – are in danger of throwing the baby out with the bathwater. Naturally, our educational initiatives should be as effective as possible, but to ask us to ignore all the research of the last few decades is akin to asking farmers to go back to milking by hand. Practical learning is real, enjoyable and lasting. After all, consider how you learn to drive a car – not by sitting in rows watching while someone explains it to you from the front of a class, followed by attempts to copy down the drawings and ideas written there, but by climbing into the driving seat and getting on with it. Of course mistakes are made, but help and advice are given by an understanding teacher. I am not suggesting that *all* learning should be of a practical nature; even using the

Artists have particular skills and perspectives which they can bring to the teaching process

car analogy, it is necessary to learn the Highway Code. But enjoyment and the best learning come from *doing*.

Who, then, are the best people to employ practical educational strategies in the most effective way? Teachers, first and foremost, of course. But an occasional partnership is worth far more than the sum of its parts. Artists in particular can be of inestimable value, not only because art is an excellent learning medium, calling for the sort of sustained observation which aids understanding and remembering, but also because artists have particular skills and perspectives which they can bring to the teaching process:

■ they have specialist knowledge which may not be available to the teacher

■ they have tremendous enthusiasm for their subject and will communicate this to children

■ they will help to make sense of an environment in visual terms, encouraging a heightened awareness of the pupil's surroundings

■ they can help with scale, positioning and the choice of media for the presentation of work

■ they demonstrate to the children that it is possible to earn one's living through the arts.

Moreover, the sharing of artistic skills encourages children's confidence in their own work and stimulates a fuller appreciation of the work of others. Children who work alongside artists forget to respond with that stock phrase, 'I can't draw'.

A residency in which practising artists are brought into contact with children will stimulate everyone in the school community – teachers, pupils, parents and the artists themselves. Everybody wins, as the examples on the following pages demonstrate.

TADPOLES

Black wriggling creatures
Struggling in muddy shadows,
Yearning to be frogs.

TREBAH PALMS

Three punk rocker trees
With spiky hair
Dance to the music of the wind
And the song of the birds.
Their faces are wrinkled,
Screwed up against the light,
And only they hear
The rhythm of the seasons
As autumn tops the charts.

Two poems written by Key Stage 2 pupils after working with poets in residence

Arts in Trust in Cornwall –
forty-five schools have been
involved since the project
began seven years ago

ARTS IN TRUST
A cross-phase project

Arts in Trust is an annual project undertaken in partnership with the National Trust, and recently sponsored by BT. It began in Cornwall seven years ago using just two properties, but has now expanded to three in the county, with similar initiatives taking place elsewhere in the country. In Cornwall alone, forty-five schools have been involved.

For one week in the spring, three artists work at each of the properties; groups of children work intensively with one artist for a full day. In addition, students and staff from the Photography Department at Falmouth School of Art work with pupils at a property on two days.

The artists' brief is to interpret the Trust site, to capture the spirit of the place. The children work practically, producing paintings, poetry, sculpture or photographs. There is always a considerable amount of follow-up work back in the classroom, and often a complete cross-curricular project is based around the classes' visit. In June the Royal Cornwall Museum in Truro hosts an exhibition of a representative selection of the children's work.

THE TREE OF LIFE
A collaborative project

The Tree of Life was undertaken in partnership with the National Trust and the Newlyn Orion Gallery, with sponsorship from Marks & Spencer. It involved four schools working on a year-long project, during which they regularly visited the Trust property of Trelissick, near Truro. Using 'the tree' as a central theme, the children studied areas of woodland near their schools, comparing them with those at Trelissick. They worked with poets, artists, sculptors and a paper maker, covering work in art, music, history, geography, mathematics and science.

The project culminated in a procession round Trelissick Gardens to which parents, governors and education staff were invited. There was also a public exhibition of work.

JOURNEYS
A project for individual classes

Journeys enabled children from thirty primary schools to plan and undertake a journey of their own, matching curriculum necessities with 'real-life' work. Pupils had to go somewhere, undertake a study while they were there and return. They were asked to make at least two visits, either to the same place or to linked sites as part of a wider project. For example, one class was studying rivers, with their local river as a focus. They planned to visit the source of the river by coach, the middle of it by boat and the mouth by train. They considered the cost of coaches, minibus hire, parental transport and train fares; they used maps and timetables and explored timing and distance; they decided on what they were going to eat for their picnics, what it would cost and how it could be provided co-operatively; they thought about safety, emergency procedures and back-up. And, of course, they pursued more traditional studies in geography, science, English, art and history.

The project was again funded by Marks & Spencer, who paid for artists, poets, writers and naturalists to work with the children on site and in the classroom. *Journeys* began with a two-day INSET course for the teachers involved, and closed with a four-week exhibition. It has since been followed by a similar project, *Seascapes*, in which children are asked to plan visits to two seaside areas, a holiday venue and a quieter natural site, contrasting the two.

COLOUR, TEXTURE, SPACE
A project for a whole school

For *Colour, Texture, Space*, we used a local 'great garden', but any open space would have done. Three artists were involved – a sculptor who was asked to look at shapes and space, and two painters, one of whom considered colour and the other texture. Each had a vertically grouped set of around thirty pupils for a whole day. They had to make sure that the children knew what they were doing because, back in school over the next three days, each group had to teach another group, particularly the practical activities.

Follow-up work back in school plays an important part in the various Arts in Trust projects

LOCAL ENVIRONMENT DAY
A project for a year group

For *Local Environment Day*, a year group of about ninety children was divided into six groups of fifteen pupils. Each group had a tutor – a geographer, a mathematician, an artist or a poet – whose brief was to study a National Trust valley with remnants of the 19th-century tin-mining industry through the area of their own expertise. The children spent the day on site with their tutors and worked back in school under the guidance of their teachers. Reports of what they had done were made by the children to the whole year group, and there was an exhibition in school for parents and visitors. ∎

Seascapes 1994 – a painting by a Key Stage 2 pupil

When the audience become the actors

Tony Jackson looks at the process of dramatising the history lesson.

Back in September last year, while preparing this article, I visited Charlecote Park in Warwickshire to observe a performance of the Young National Trust Theatre's *For Any Field?*, a drama that focussed on events connected with the movement to set up the National Trust in 1895. The moment I particularly recollect – and one that caused me (yet again) to overhaul my views about this kind of work – was the culminating sequence of the afternoon. The pupils in their various groups converged on the Great Hall to debate the pros and cons of a proposal to sell part of the estate to the county council for building new homes for slum-dwellers from nearby Birmingham. The debate was heated, the issues were difficult and the various points of view were each perfectly defensible yet problematic. The pupils were utterly absorbed.

As a seasoned observer of educational theatre, I have always believed that experiences such as this must be underpinned by a strong element of theatricality. But how far, if at all, did theatrical art have any part to play in what was going on here? For these pupils at this moment, the theatre seemed at first glance irrelevant. The arguments were 'real'. The characters were human beings with specific standpoints, who needed to be won over or supported. It could almost have been a lively classroom debate or a public meeting. The earlier, more overtly theatrical parts of the narrative had been overtaken by events as a sense of crisis loomed and the level of the pupils' involvement intensified. Reality had seemed to replace realism.

Was this a drama, or a history lesson, or both? Had the theatre simply been a means of engaging the children, to be relegated to the background when it was no longer needed? How important to the success of the event were the costumes, the fictitious characterisations and the extraordinary setting? When you can no longer see the usual dividing lines between actor and audience, when the audience seem to become the actors, what kind of theatre is being practised?

Yet it was evident that these young people were involved in something much more than just another debate. Despite the reality of the dispute, they were arguing within a specific historical framework. The trains were not electric but steam-driven, noisy and dirty. Working on a farm was neither automated nor as idyllic as city-dwellers imagine. You could not advise someone living in appalling housing to appeal to the Department of Social Security. Perhaps the historic setting, the costumes, the distinctiveness of the characters and the views they embodied, *were* still playing an active part, sustaining a very particular world and providing a reminder of it as and when needed.

A natural setting

What exactly was the value of the location? After all, the piece was not strictly site-specific: the YNTT move around every couple of weeks to a different property in a different part of the

FOR ANY FIELD? – how important are the costumes, the fictitious characterisations and the extraordinary setting?

country. But even if the plot and characters remain the same from place to place, from the *pupils'* point of view the house is inevitably perceived as the natural setting for the events they witness – integrally related to the stories, people and arguments they encounter within it. The complex texture of the social fabric, the status and jobs of the various characters, the question of whose territory we're on and where power resides – all will influence the course of the debate and the pupils' grasp of the period. No longer is historical fact kept separate from ordinary lives and concerns.

The YNTT's work is pioneering and important – but it has not emerged from nowhere. It has its roots firmly embedded in the Theatre-in-Education movement which began in Britain in the mid-1960s. And, arguably, the company now constitutes one of the country's leading exponents of the 'classic' form of TiE – the fully-participatory programme.

So what is Theatre-in-Education? It might best be defined as the use of theatre for explicitly educational purposes, closely allied to the curriculum and usually taking place in educational contexts – schools, colleges, youth clubs, museums and historic sites. It tends to be a highly portable form of theatre, using minimal sets and lighting, but practised by professional specialist companies, people who possess both educational and acting skills and who aim to bring high quality performance work into the classroom or school hall.

Interaction

Above all, TiE will usually involve some element of interaction with the audience. It may be a short play followed by a workshop in which actors and children together will explore some of the issues further, using techniques such as the 'hot-seating' (cross-examination) of characters from the play or the replaying and analysis of decisive moments of the action; or it may – for younger children especially – involve the active participation of the children in role throughout. Whatever the age or format, young people do not watch simply as passive spectators; they engage with the events they witness.

The philosophy which underpins this work stems from the belief that *learning is enhanced by doing*; that, in role, pupils are likely to engage at a different and often more intense level than is usual in the classroom; and that their interest in

When the audience become the actors, what kind of theatre is being practised?

and understanding of the issues, events and characters involved will thus be enhanced. Its efficacy is indisputable, but most would agree that its importance and impact are difficult to convey fully to anyone who has not witnessed it.

Ever since its inception, TiE in Britain has relied heavily on public subsidy for its survival. In recent years, however, as government has pushed to make everything – education and the arts included – subject to the rigours of the market-place, the ability of TiE companies to operate with the small audience sizes necessary for the full impact of the experience has come under enormous strain. Many companies have had to close, while others have had to play to ever-larger audiences, and there is no doubt that there has been some dilution of TiE practice in recent years.

But good innovative work still goes on. The YNTT is fortunate not only in being allied to an organisation such as the National Trust but in benefitting from the sponsorship that this alliance has attracted. This has not removed the burden from schools, who must still pay (at a subsidised rate) for the opportunities offered, but it is significant that they value the work enough to continue booking the company even during times of ever-tightening budgets.

This freedom from conventional funding sources, together with its brief to animate the history that has passed through the National Trust's many properties, has allowed the YNTT to remain a standard-bearer for a unique kind of TiE experience – evolved in Britain, valued by educationists, threatened by cuts in funding yet still envied in many countries around the world. Long may this vital work continue to flourish. ■

SUE MAYO

The touring performance

Writer-director Sue Mayo explains what is involved in devising a Young National Trust Theatre production.

The Young National Trust Theatre aims to bring alive a period of history in a challenging and thought-provoking manner, in a way which also breathes life into the properties where it performs. The children are swept up in a drama which demands their involvement. Through the different characters whom they meet, each one carrying a different strand of human experience, the play creates a world in which the children can gain real insights into what people thought and feared, what their passions were, the details of their lives. A nine-year-old boy who visited Charlecote in Warwickshire several months

AN ENDLESS MAZE – Catholics and Protestants in the Counter-Reformation at Osterley Park, Middlesex

after his experience as a 1920s schoolboy in the YNTT's *A Land Fit for Heroes?* (1991) walked up to a puzzled room steward: 'Don't you remember me? I was in a play here.' Clearly that one visit should have been as much a highlight for others as it had been for him.

As a writer, one of my most exciting and challenging tasks has been to choose the characters who will carry the key elements in the chosen period. We can all make assumptions about the men and women of the past, and

often imagine them to have fitted rather neatly into boxes – roundhead or cavalier, royalist or republican, capitalist or communist. However, one soon discovers all sorts of ambiguous characters often hidden from the history books – like, for example, the many Tudor parish priests who managed to survive persecution of both Protestants and Catholics, quietly shifting their allegiance until more settled times.

In *An Endless Maze* (1992), set during the Counter-Reformation, children met the head of the household, Sir William Vyse, a loyal Catholic who was enjoying the opportunity to be fully involved in public life. With him lived his sister, Edith, once a nun. When her convent was closed down in Edward VI's time, Edith chose to return to live with her family. From her, the children had a personal account of the destruction of a way of life. Also living with Sir William was his niece Grace, a young woman on the brink of adult life – but with very different choices from the young women of today. A visitor to the house was a Spanish cloth merchant, Ramon Gomez. He held out the chance of new money coming to the neighbourhood, but he also encountered the immense hostility of local people to foreigners, especially the Spanish. A pedlar, Simon Luckham, brought ribbons and buttons and, more importantly, news from other villages. He also carried a secret – he was a Protestant, and in constant danger as Mary Tudor tried to suppress the reformers.

These were the characters whom the children met, with whom they interacted. Through them they gained knowledge and insight, but they also encountered some unanswered questions. Each character had his or her own complexities and point of view. Yet each had to try to open up to the children the wider context of the period and the central, underlying issues. Through meeting and talking with people whose lives were affected and challenged by the events of the time, the children were encouraged to ask the same questions for themselves.

Central roles

The narrative of a piece of history-based TiE must sweep the participants along, so that their curiosity is aroused, their desire to know more is kept alive, and a connection is made with what those children really feel is important, what they care about. It is interesting to note how hard it is for children now to understand the centrality of religion and the importance of denomination which runs so deeply through British history. I can remember an exasperated youngster exploding, 'What does it matter what you believe? I don't believe anything !' She could not imagine why anyone would choose to die for a religious belief. Yet, in the same play, as actors and children debated the fate of the Protestant pedlar, another child stood up, flushed with emotion, to say, 'I am a Catholic, but I would die for this man.'

The children's own roles are central to the play. Taking on a role helps them to make a bridge between their own experience and that of the people living in the period they will 'visit'.

But that role cannot be rehearsed. In school, pupils can prepare the ground carefully, imagining what life might have been like as a 16th-century villager, as a schoolchild in the 1920s, or as a Victorian philanthropist. They can take on new names, prepare costumes, create a family and a biography for their character. All of this makes a good foundation

for work in role. Yet the role only really comes to life in the moments of interaction with the actors.

Watching the cast working with the children at the start of a show is fascinating. Often you'll see a child hesitating before plunging into a new world. This is the moment when he or she consents to be involved, and it is a crucial one.

When in *An Endless Maze* one of the characters greeted a group of sixty children who constituted the local villagers, she first had to get their agreement to marching on Sir William's house in a protest about rents. 'Do you *all* say "aye"? Nay, I must hear you all say "aye".' With their first tentative or enthusiastic 'aye' the children were off, and the next question – 'How many bales of cloth do you have that you cannot sell?' – was met with a quick response. For those who cannot opt in so quickly, there must be opportunities throughout the play to do so, and participation need not only be measured by verbal involvement. As Dorothy Heathcote once said, one of the joys of theatre is 'the right to stare'.

The actors must stick solidly to their roles, equipped with a secure knowledge about their character and the historical context of the play. They constantly encourage the children in their roles, reinforcing what they already know, and encouraging them to express their views. In the YNTT's *Virtues and Vanities* (1993), which was set

The Dragon Dance from
AN ENDLESS MAZE — music and
dance play a vital part in
the action

in 1680, a child in role as a wealthy gentleman became extremely concerned about the safety of King Charles. 'For goodness sake, phone him!', he cried. Rather than pointing out the anachronism, the actor supported the child's call, recognising that this boy really was in role and expressing his desire for urgency in the first words that came to hand.

When deciding on the role which the children will take, it is essential to find one which will enable them to make a connection with the issues of the play. One way to do this is to put them directly in the path of those issues so that their characters will be affected by them.

In *A Land Fit for Heroes?* the children were asked to come as the leavers' class from the local village school, invited on an annual outing to the 'Big House'. Preparation included researching what they would have been studying at school and how they would have learned. What were the possibilities for them as they prepared to leave school at fourteen? What were their aspirations? Through the characters they met in the play they were introduced to a wider view of the period: the impact of the Great War, the General Strike, the 'servant problem', the influence of the USA, the right to vote and the

shortage of jobs. Within this wider picture the schoolchildren discovered that the Big House was to be sold – the family was bankrupt. Something which everyone thought would never change was about to disappear, and this would have a major effect on the whole community. Given the chance to talk to the family about what had happened, the children responded in different ways:

■ 'This is change at the expense of a lot of people.'

■ 'Everything's got to change. In the long run it may be a change for the better. We just can't see it now.'

■ 'My father is the smith, and if you go he may lose his employment. I had hoped to follow in his footsteps. Why can't you sell your London house and stay here?'

The children were using their own experience and judgement to see things from another person's point of view, standing in the shoes of a rural child of the 1920s. Interestingly, it was not a question of acting – that can sometimes get in the way. It was about the child's ability to respond in role to the stimulus of character and action – an extension of imaginative play.

Children themselves are aware of the pleasure of this kind of learning. As one participant pointed out afterwards: 'I thought it was a brilliant idea, because I think children are more prepared to learn if they're actually doing something that's really good fun.'

Within a good TiE production pupils are encouraged to help to influence decisions, to gather information and to draw conclusions – although it can sometimes be a struggle to maintain authenticity when the children's decision might, as it were, change history. In *Virtues and Vanities* the group advised Phillida, a young Catholic woman, on whether to accept a marriage proposal from Mr Scattergood, a Protestant merchant. In the early performances, the actors followed the majority decision, whatever it was. But it soon became clear to us that, given her circumstances, Phillida really had to marry her merchant. So while we continued to ask the children's opinion, we sometimes had to disappoint those who had advised her against, believing that this gave a more accurate if less comfortable understanding of a woman's choices in 1680. (This did not prevent an eight-year-old admirer from inundating Phillida with love letters afterwards, in the hope of getting her to change her mind.)

Set piece

A character in the play that should never be underestimated is the house itself. Performing in a medieval manor house, an Elizabethan tithe barn or a baroque palace can add an essential ingredient to the whole experience. When the children see a character lean out of the window to call them, or follow the butler into the kitchens, or hear an argument through a closed door, or dance in the courtyard, any sense of the house as museum is gone.

Sometimes, of course, children can be overwhelmed by the size and impact of the buildings, and here the wearing of costume can help them to feel less foreign to their surroundings. If initially the house simply represents to them a place that is grand, that is 'other', they soon begin to pick up its significance in the particular period being presented. It might be a hiding place or an ostentatious symbol of power. Some of the characters belong there, others don't. Some belong above stairs, others below. By the end of a performance – ninety minutes in the company of the house – the children have often had a very privileged and familiar view of it, and can no longer doubt, if they ever did, that people lived here.

Theatre is by its very nature a collaborative art form. As a writer, I see and hear my words interpreted by actors. Musicians, dancers, stage manager and designers also have a part to play in creating the whole. The work of the YNTT takes this sense of collaboration further, the play working in partnership with the lively and robust element of participation from the children, and the fascinating challenge of adapting to the powerful personalities of the houses. I, for one, do not doubt that the most powerful learning comes through experience, and history-based TiE in a period setting provides a rich arena for both learning and experience. ■

Mr Stone, the butler in A LAND FIT FOR HEROES?, at Polesden Lacey in Surrey

Performing arts and inner city schools

Liz Rothschild has devised and directed several performing arts projects at Sutton House in Hackney. Honor Rhone talked to her about the most recent residency.

In the early 1990s, the National Trust decided to expand its history through drama programme by inaugurating a series of Performing Arts in Trust residencies at various Trust properties. PAITs, as they have become known, differ from both conventional living history and the sort of history-based TiE practised by the Young National Trust Theatre, in that they give children the opportunity to work intensively with professional actors over a period of several days. As a result there is a much greater emphasis on pupils as originators, creators who devise their own work and decide what form it will take.

Liz Rothschild, who has worked as both actor and artistic director with the Young National Trust Theatre, has devised several PAITs with Key Stage 2 pupils. The mechanics, as she describes them, seem straightforward enough:

■ A class of pupils is introduced to the property by a small group of actors who tour the house with the children, guiding their thoughts with specific questions.

■ The actors spend a day with the pupils in school. The company performs a short scripted piece which lasts for fifteen or twenty minutes – a plank, as Liz describes it, on which to rest a great deal of historical information, so that the pupils are grounded in the chosen theme. After a short debate over some of the issues which the piece has raised, actors and children begin to devise creative responses to those issues; the dramatic sequences which evolve come very clearly out of the relationship between child and actor.

■ A second day is spent at the property itself, working up the pieces that the children have devised, usually with a single member of the company.

■ Finally the class returns to the property with participants from a second school which has been working in tandem with the actors. After rehearsals, both schools perform their pieces before an invited audience of parents and teachers.

Liz Rothschild during a Performing Arts in Trust residency at Sutton House, Hackney, in 1993

An intense experience

This outline does no justice to the intensity of the experience and the process involved. Liz's first project was based at Sutton House in Hackney. The schools involved had a high proportion of children from minority cultures; and the PAIT focused on the idea of foreign-ness and alienation. Rooted in the sixteenth century, it grew out of a short play in which four characters – an African prince who had been brought to the capital, a merchant, a sea captain and a maidservant who had migrated to London from the West Country – explored what it was like to be a stranger in a strange land. Pupils were split into four groups, each working with a single character to produce scenes that arose out of how they imagined other scenes from that character's life. This in itself was quite challenging: 'It was interesting to see that the children always took the prince back to Africa', says Liz. 'They wanted to place him, to give him back his power.'

Neither the company nor the children used costumes of any kind. Liz feels that the pupils' time is better spent on creative work: 'If *we* wear costume, it is as if we're saying to the children, "This is how we make it work, we rely on these things to transform us. Now you're going to do it without." I don't want that dissonance.' But emblematic props did form part of the creative process. The actors themselves carried large paper symbols – a big paper ruff, a huge quill – and then invited the children to choose a single object to make and bring to the performance. 'The notion was that you don't need money or fancy costumes or a lot of resources to transform your reality.'

Education for all

Liz's most recent project focused on the late Victorians, as part of the National Trust's 1995 Centenary celebrations. She began by looking for another subject which would be immediately relevant to a multicultural group. But the sort of treatment that had worked so well in the previous PAIT, a black character coping with living in Elizabethan England, didn't really gel; and she soon became excited about another area of common experience – education. Like its predecessor, the 1995 PAIT went beyond basic history, exploring some of the problems that compulsory education posed for working-class families who relied on the

income brought home by their children. 'I liked the notion that a whole generation of working-class children were becoming literate. I saw in that a power and a mobility, a way in which children could play a fuller part in society.' Liz was also intrigued by the parallels with modern-day children from ethnic minorities whose parents may still be uncomfortable with English.

The central character in the short set-piece is a child whose father is suspicious of the power that education will bring, and anxious at the loss of both control within the family and income. 'It is that conflict between the outer world of

society and the traditional family hierarchy – the state can now say, "Your child *will* go to school. We are more powerful than you."'

Within this general framework, the children worked with visual primary sources from the period, creating 'befores' and 'afters' to late nineteenth-century photographs which drew out aspects of the central theme. They also devised riddles and stories based around Victorian props, created movement and sound sequences, and even experimented with techniques from Victorian melodrama.

The PAIT was an undoubted success, with the children responding creatively and sensitively to difficult issues, and originating work rather than having ideas imposed upon them. When asked what she wanted pupils to gain from the project, Liz said, 'I want them to come away with a lively experience of what it is to relate to history through performance. And I want them to find their own performer in themselves.'

Both of these objectives were achieved. ∎

'I want children to find their own performer in themselves'

RICHARD W. HARRIS

Talking furniture, whispering arches

Richard W. Harris gives a teacher's perspective on Performing Arts in Trust.

My initial reaction on receiving an invitation for my school to take part in a YNTT Performing Arts in Trust session was interest, tinged with a degree of hesitation. Taking thirty Year 10 pupils out of school for two days requires a good deal of planning, funding, organising – and tact, where one's colleagues are concerned. However, the project proved to be an enormously rewarding experience for me and the pupils, overcoming any trepidation felt during the early stages.

The decision to include the Year 10 Drama option group in the PAIT at Sutton House was based on an attempt to place them immediately in a project that required a firm deadline. This was to be the first project of their two-year Drama GCSE option course and most of the pupils had not worked together before. It would be an opportunity for them to experience working with a new group, alongside pupils from another school, in an intensive project. It was to be two days of fun, good humour and concentrated work that culminated in a successful performance for parents and friends.

Until its recent restoration, Sutton House appears to have hidden itself amongst the neighbouring changes and developments, quietly gathering its catalogue of histories and secrets. Its renovation has exposed various aspects of that organic development and they have been left as markers of the changes of use – Tudor courtier's house, dame school, church institute, offices and, until recently, a squat. The challenge for the pupils was to see if they could express this history and interpret their reactions to it using music, drama and movement.

The pupils' first morning of workshops was a mixture of nervousness, excitement, adolescent knowingness, and a trepidation about meeting the boys from the partner school. I suspect this temporary partnership was promoted by a shared feeling of how clever the participants were to choose an option that gave you an authorised two-day absence from school, and perhaps also a concern over the amount of commitment that would be required over the next two days.

What sort of animal?

An unaccompanied discovery tour was the pupils' first introduction to Sutton House. They explored the building independently, making notes on their impressions with the aid of a questionnaire which asked questions such as: 'If the house were an animal, what sort of animal would it be?' and 'Which room has the most uncomfortable atmosphere?' This created an immediate intimacy, a sense of ownership of the house. On their return to their main working area, the Wenlock Barn, pupils spoke about the objects and rooms with an assured familiarity that they might apply to the latest school gossip. Many talked about the echoes of footsteps on the wooden floorboards, the creaking of the thick oak doors, and the heavy metallic clunk of the doorlatches – elements that would later feature in their music and storytelling performance. They almost all identified the cellar as the dampest, smelliest, creepiest, most

The challenge for pupils is to interpret their reactions to the past through music, drama and movement – Performing Arts in Trust, 1994

unpleasant area, a place where they would certainly not like to be left alone in – mixed emotions, as it also contained a visible yet secure area which held the wine cellar of the Sutton House restaurant.

While the pupils adjourned to the local McDonalds for lunch, the five workshop leaders sifted through their notebooks and developed the pupils' thoughts into a promenade performance that was intended to last for about an hour. During the afternoon session the two schools, Langdon Park and Homerton House, were mixed into approximately seven groups. Each group was allocated a station around the house where the following day they would use their writings to present an aspect of their thoughts on the atmosphere within the house.

Promenade performance

The next day, an invited audience was shown an introductory sequence on what secrets the house might hold. Thereafter the performance became a promenade, as throughout the house the roving audience introduced to a variety of activities ranging from storytelling and 'thought shadowing' on the encroachment of the city, to a secret whispering group who moved around the house, forming 'whispering arches' up one of the stairwells and silently intermingling with the audience like the ghosts of schoolchildren from its time as a boarding school. Percussion instruments were combined with the sounds of children playing in the courtyard, an indication of how time and the rhythm of history had marked the progress of Sutton House.

The audience's tour finished with a performance back in the Wenlock Barn. This included a movement piece using screens of gauze stretched across canes, which were moved both vertically and horizontally as the group peered around and moved among them until the gauze walls closed slowly around like a Wendy House, creating a familiarity and intimacy amongst the mixed inter-school group that was quite remarkable. Recitals of poetry written by the pupils were accompanied by freeze-frames symbolising different aspects of the house. Talking pieces of furniture, formed by the pupils' bodies, commented on how they had been treated over the years. By the finale, a song entitled *Memories of the Past*, I was convinced that the Langdon Park Drama Group had undergone a tiring but fulfilling experience.

What secrets does Sutton House hold?

Back at school, drama lessons were approached with a greater awareness of how much work is involved in a presentation. There was also a sense of pride amongst the pupils over their achievement. The project had managed to fix Sutton House's unique atmosphere in the minds of the children. They came away with a realisation that atmosphere and its creation are intrinsic elements in any group performance.

The anecdotal phase of the performance soon began to fade, but the memory of the experience and the intimacy that the participants felt with Sutton House still affects their work. They have maintained an individual sense of responsibility towards the group, which helps them in their performance skills. They are appreciative of the value of rehearsal. And they have developed a broader awareness of the possible diversity of the arts and their potential for communicating to an audience. ■

Directing history-based TiE

Honor Rhone talks to the YNTT's current artistic director Matthew Townshend.

'We're not asking the children to do living history. We're not saying, "Come to a YNTT show and you'll find out what it was like to scrub floors and blacklead the grates." Pupils have to engage at an intellectual level with some very complex historical issues. We're asking an awful lot of them – and we usually get it.'

Matthew Townshend, the Young National Trust Theatre's artistic director, is well qualified to know how far history-based Theatre-in-Education can push children – and how much it can achieve. With a background in TiE, children's theatre and community arts, Townshend joined the YNTT in 1994, devising and directing *The Tree Grows Still*, in which the action took place during the final months of the Commonwealth. Since then he has been responsible, among other

FOR ANY FIELD? – in the areas of the play that are improvised, the actor comes in close with the children

things, for directing John Harrison's *For Any Field?*, the YNTT's celebration of the National Trust's Centenary which investigated some of the social and environmental problems that led to the founding of the Trust in 1895; *A Very Big Thing*, the National Trust/National Gallery pantomime which was also based on the origins of the Trust; and the company's most recent show, *Flowers and Slaves*, which focuses on the marriage of Victoria and Albert in 1840.

For Townshend, the process of enabling children to get to grips with the social and political issues of the past is vital. The choice of period is thus inextricably bound up with identifying the historical concerns that will form the core of the drama. The dictates of the history curriculum may govern the choice in its broadest terms – the Victorians and the Tudors are clear favourites for a company that works chiefly with pupils at Key Stage 2 – but within this general framework there is usually an embarrassment of riches, and the problem lies in deciding what to discard.

'It's easy to clutter a ninety-minute performance by setting too many hares running', says Townshend. Children who participate in a YNTT performance aren't coming to take part in a typical day in the life of a country house in 1659, or 1895, or whenever. There must always be a crunch issue, a crisis that will be reached and that will directly involve them. 'They must never be allowed to wander round following the action, thinking "This is exciting. What they will do next?" They have to think, "What will we do next?".'

In *The Tree Grows Still*, for example, pupils were asked to arrive in role as members of one of three social groups – gentry, tradespeople and radical artisans. With Oliver Cromwell recently dead and his son Richard clearly not up to the job of governing the country, each of these groups would hold a view on the central question – 'What do we do now?' In role, the children were encouraged to think about the options – the restoration of the monarchy, a new republic with checks and balances to prevent one person taking too much power, the dismantling of established institutions in favour of community-based people's councils. The children had already researched the social group to which they belonged and decided where their allegiances might lie. But the drama not only reinforced their own sense of who their characters were, what they might want; it also gave them to chance to talk through the implications of their characters' choices, to see that sometimes there are no right and wrong answers.

The radical artisans, for instance, were all for dispensing completely with central government. But they were encouraged to look at what this might mean. How should they organise themselves? What if other members of society didn't agree with them? There is nothing wrong, thinks Townshend, with rocking the children's world a little, making them see that life in the past was much more complicated than the textbooks sometimes suggest.

Past and present

The outcome was dictated by history, of course. Whatever they decided, Charles II would be restored to the throne. The children may have known this, but the characters they played did not. This tension between past and present extends beyond an awareness that whatever one may decide in the context of the drama, events will – already have – turned out in a certain way. The world in which we live conspires against a child's natural ability to become someone else, sometimes quite dramatically; when the YNTT was working at Cragside in Northumberland recently, each performance was regularly interrupted by the sound of jets flying overhead.

At other times, though, the process is more subtle than a low-flying Tornado. In *For Any Field?* says Townshend, the children were asked to make some difficult decisions about environmental issues. The show centred on the clash between the desire of some Victorians to improve people's living conditions and the effect that indiscriminate development was having on the landscape. Pupils were familiar with environmental concerns, but they approached those concerns from a very modern standpoint. For them, animals were as important as human beings, and animal welfare counted just as strongly as human welfare. 'This just wouldn't have figured in the thinking of Victorian reformers. Animals didn't matter; it was the betterment of humankind that counted. We had to try to lead the children to see that *For Any Field?* wasn't about "green" issues in the way that the late 20th century sees them.'

This is usually achieved through the interaction between actor and child. 'In the areas of the play that are improvised, there is the opportunity for the actor to come in close with the kids and then to draw them back. One encourages them to articulate their concerns, and leads them gently to see that they aren't part of the game – "You're talking about things that I don't understand."'

So is contemporary relevance important? After all, surely there are some obvious parallels to be drawn between Victorian conservationists and modern-day environmentalists, or between the uncertainties surrounding the monarchy at the time of Queen Victoria's marriage and the current state of the royal family?

'Of course there are,' says Townshend. 'But it is our job to point children in those directions without stepping out of the historical frame. If we start to disrupt that frame, the kids could say, "Hang on – you've asked us to believe that this is 1895, or 1840, and we've done our best. But now you are breaking the contract".'

And in spite of the importance that he places on historical issues, Townshend sees the significance of history-based TiE in other terms. 'Time and again, teachers tell us that the value of what we do lies far beyond our role as a history-based company. It lies in the fact that children learn to talk with rather than at their peers. They learn to work together and to discuss problems. They come to see that their view of the world is not the only view.' ■

In THE TREE GROWS STILL, Townshend encouraged children to see that life in the past was more complicated than the textbooks suggest

The primary school experience

Steven Hales assesses the impact of a Young National Trust Theatre performance.

'It's an experience you have to catch.'

That was the reaction of one ten-year-old after visiting Wimpole Hall, Cambridgeshire, and working with the Young National Trust Theatre. She had obviously revelled in all aspects of the show: the preparatory work, creating her own character; the excitement of the visit itself, where she interacted with the characters in the story; and the period of reflection back in the classroom.

Schools have an important role in bringing heritage and history into the lives of young people. Interestingly, from my class of ten- and eleven-year-olds, only twelve out of thirty-two thought they had visited places of historical interest with their parents. Fortunately, many schools – and particularly primary schools – adopt a policy of using the community as a learning resource and visiting historic sites is an important part of that process.

The National Curriculum

The National Curriculum sets out the areas of historical study and the key elements of chronology, range and depth of knowledge and understanding, historical interpretation, historical inquiry, and organisation and communication. It is the role of the teacher to plan experiences which will bring their teaching to life so that the children will learn and remember. The whole movement of 'bringing history to life' is an important resource, and productions by companies like the Young National Trust Theatre are fundamental to this process.

Much more than history is involved, however, because many primary school teachers will incorporate other aspects of the curriculum into their planning – English, music, art, religious education – perhaps creating a large cross-curricular project which will run for half a term or more.

Before, during and after

Curriculum planning takes place early in primary schools. It is important that whoever sifts through the post links the wealth of resources that are available on the open market to curriculum plans which may look two or three years ahead. When the Young National Trust Theatre flyer arrives, it is important to act quickly, checking curriculum links, consulting with the history co-ordinator and class teachers, and making the bookings. Once the date has been fixed, the YNTT's resource book is a vital element to support teachers' planning.

In the weeks prior to the actual production, teacher and pupils begin their preparations, allocating their characters, seeking out relationships and exploring how the community functions, starting to build the background to the story and creating their costume. In some cases, the musical elements of the production will be rehearsed.

When the day of the performance finally comes round, the children's excitement is high but, having arrived at the site, they are awed by their surroundings. They soon start to relax, however, once they meet the actors and the story begins to unfold. Their confidence grows and they

Schools have an important role in bringing heritage and history into the lives of young people

begin to participate. When the interaction between the characters is in full flow, the children grow into their characters and into the story; they become animated and totally involved. The YNTT's actor-teachers are skilled in bringing the children out of themselves.

In a number of productions, the denouement comes about as a debate and it is here that the children shine through with their enthusiasm for the debate and their sense of natural justice. On the coach journey home the debate continues – and continues, and continues.

Back in the classroom the children are ready for all kinds of follow-up. It may be character studies or it may be further research. Research does excite the children, especially when it involves people and places. My own class worked with the YNTT at Wimpole Hall in 1995, when the Centenary show, *For Any Field?*, featured Octavia Hill. The children knew that Octavia had a local connection and they contacted the chairperson of the Octavia Hill Society. He was invited to the school and the children interviewed him. As they were keen on electronic mail and fax links, they went on to communicate with the Octavia Hill Society of Pennsylvania to assist them with their research.

The culmination of such work is often a definite product – perhaps a project book or an exhibition of work, or even a recreation of the drama. In one school where I have worked, the whole school community returned to Charlecote Park and recreated the story of the Lucy family, with the head teacher taking the role of Lady Lucy and the school cook playing the housekeeper.

Books or living history?

My class debated the issue of which was more important, books or living history, and resolved that both played an important part in the teaching and learning of history. One of the children said that living history gives you 'a real picture in your head', while another said that books gave you information against which you can check out your own ideas. One of the children mentioned that information from books can be biased, and that a TiE production enabled you to 'make your own judgements'.

How schools spend their financial resources is a management debate but, if your school is committed to experiential learning, it is my belief that investing in the resources of people and places brings the curriculum to life. ∎

When the interaction is in full flow, the children grow into their characters and into the story

Working with the YNTT

Simon Hutchens gives an actor's view of Theatre-in-Education.

Under the shade of a large tree and within sight of the big house, I stand with a group of fifteen young people from a local primary school. Today they are Victorian factory workers from the city, complete with collarless shirts and dark trousers, flat caps and heavy boots. I put on my own flat cap and scan their expectant faces before I begin to speak.

Simon Hutchens in TWO NATIONS at Charlecote Park, Warwickshire, in 1990

My aim is not to entertain them as an audience en masse, but to seek out individual reaction and group interaction as I travel with them on an educational journey. From the outset it is impossible to predict exactly how much each one of them will become involved in the drama. Every child presents a unique challenge for the team of actor-teachers working on a participatory Theatre-in-Education programme.

The function of an actor

At the beginning of a TiE performance, the participants may be shy, overawed, nervous about the nature of their impending participation. The first actor to meet them faces a difficult task: not only will his or her character proclaim the style of the theatrical experience, but he or she must also begin to ask questions of the young people in role, setting the tone for the type of participation expected of them in the rest of the programme. In a well-crafted show, this task is made a little easier because the first character that pupils meet is generally one to whom they can relate quite easily. More than likely, it will be a someone from the same socio-economic background, who may even be dressed in a similar fashion.

The actor must not only convincingly tell their character's story but also continue to ask more and more probing questions of the participants, progressing from simple details about their family and work, to soliciting their opinions and reactions to 'recent' events. As well as trying to elicit each individual's commitment and some evidence of their understanding, one needs to foster a sense of group identity. A good group dynamic will feed an individual's work in role, encouraging them to respect their peer group as role models. It will help to bridge a potential divide, if pupils have come together from two or more different schools. And it will provide a constructive forum for any debate and decision-making still to come in the programme.

Members of a group may be shy, or one or two more confident individuals may tend to dominate. Some will be desperate to show the extent of their knowledge of the period by attempting to answer every question, while others might challenge the 'reality' of the situation with funny answers or unsolicited suggestions. An actor must have all his or her improvisational skills at hand in order to keep the programme moving forward while remaining in character.

Within the narrative structure of most YNTT performances, there is usually some consideration and discussion in small groups of a final question. Up to this point the actors have worked to deepen the participants' sense of working in role. Questions have been answered by characters in order to promote understanding and to avoid confusion, without over-simplifying the issues. In this final arena, the actors must make sure that the children feel that their presence, their opinions and their input are vital to any resolution or as part of any ongoing debate. A good debate will include a variety of interactions, between participants and characters, participants from different groups or even their own group, and between characters. Such debates are not scripted – now, more than at any other point in the programme, the actors must be alert, not only supporting the children but also presenting and reacting to fresh challenges and questions. I remember how during one rather lacklustre debate, I jumped to my feet and challenged the actor leading another group, accusing his character of dishonesty and a lack of commitment to solving the problems at hand. Angry and exasperated, my character was all for giving up, but the young people around me challenged my despondency and re-entered the debate with renewed vigour.

A final point about the function of the actor – in the early stages of the tour it is vital that the cast share their objective appraisal of the programme with the director and with each other. Even after extensive rehearsals and tech runs at each venue, it is difficult to predict which elements of a programme will be effective and which may need reworking. In a YNTT show, where several groups are working simultaneously around a property, it will be some time before the director will have seen all the elements of the programme. The actors' feedback is essential for any evaluation.

Preparation and rehearsal

Prior to the beginning of rehearsals, the actors will have been given the exact year in which the programme is set, the major issues on which they will focus, and an outline of their characters. My own approach is to look at two areas of research which are closely interlinked – the historical events and issues both at the time of and immediately preceding the period in question, and the effect of those events on a human level – how people's lives were changed and how they felt about that change.

History books in the children's section of any good library are a valuable resource. They are the same type of material that the participants will be using for research and they are written for a specific age group. It is useful to note which historical issues are pinpointed and the method and language used to explain their cause and effect. I have also found it useful to scan children's history books, both text and illustrations, for the more bizarre or unusual snippet of information. This is just the sort of thing that a child will use to impress you with, or question you on, during a show.

The adult library can give more specific information, including discussions on the causes and effects of events, the art and

An actor must have all his or her improvisational skills at hand to keep the programme moving forward – VIRTUES AND VANITIES at Belton House in Lincolnshire, 1993

Actors bring the ability to play to an audience, some of whom are no more than a metre away

ACTORS, TEACHERS AND ACTOR-TEACHERS

The YNTT company is composed of actor-teachers. Although we have chosen theatre as our medium for education, we use skills from both professions.

THE ACTOR'S SKILLS

■ good improvisational skills to cope with the unexpected

■ the ability to play to an audience, some of whom are no more than a metre away

■ the ability to make a character approachable enough that participants will feel able to ask questions, even if the character is not 'friendly' towards them

■ the ability to move smoothly from acting in a scene to facilitating a discussion to teaching a dance or a song

■ the ability to work indoors and outdoors in very different acoustic environments

■ the ability to adapt to the different layouts of a series of venues

■ the ability to memorise fine-weather and wet-weather versions of a performance

THE TEACHER'S SKILLS

■ devising and posing questions clearly

■ gauging participants' levels of understanding and involvement, not only by their answers but also by their *lack* of answers, their physicality and their attentiveness

■ the ability to ensure that all are able to contribute and are encouraged to do so; hence an awareness of those who dominate and those who hide

■ the ability to alternate between open questions which require more than a yes/no answer, and closed questions which need a quick decision

■ simple crowd control, both when moving around a property and when trying to see and hear everyone during group discussions

literature of the period, and biographies. This research is useful when considering a specific character in his or her historical setting.

During rehearsals, the actors use their research combined with information given in the script to build on their knowledge of their characters' histories. Decisions are made as to their opinion on recent events, even those events considered to be outside the scope of the programme. Within rehearsals the dramatic impact and usefulness to pupils of such information can be assessed.

This sort of material is useful for a number of reasons. The nature of a YNTT programme, for example, requires that the actors stay in character throughout. Obviously an in-depth knowledge of the character as well as a firm grasp of the structure of the programme can help in any necessary improvisation. It can also help when answering personal questions a participant may ask, sometimes in genuine curiosity, sometimes as a way of testing you. The material can be introduced outside the script, as a private aside to an individual or perhaps as an extra piece of group theatre or storytelling. The actor may decide that this is just the thing to encourage a desultory group, or to further stimulate children who are already involved.

During rehearsals for *A Land Fit for Heroes?* (1991), the director and I decided that my character had two children, one of whom was a talented musician. This was a source of both joy and bitterness to the character; he was proud of his child's talent yet could not afford to buy an instrument for her. This seemingly inconsequential point could be shared with the group as we moved from one room to another. Perhaps it would be linked to a child's reference to the wealthy surroundings, or be triggered by an individual's in-role response when questioned about their own family.

The country house setting

For some participants, a YNTT show is perhaps their first visit to this particular property. For others it may be their first visit to any country house. The actor can often capitalise on the sense of wonder and curiosity to illustrate both his or her own status and that of the participants. I have seen some children open-mouthed in awe at their surroundings, while others are blasé. Both responses are challenges for the actor.

Blickling Hall, Norfolk – the actor can often capitalise on the sense of wonder and curiosity produced by the country house setting

There are some features of an historic house which break the illusion, like 'Do Not Touch' signs, areas that are roped off, and the presence of room stewards and members of the public. The actor must be aware of all these things and either ignore them or, in the worst cases, compete with them by increasing the element of drama to keep the participants' attention.

Children – and teachers – can sometimes inadvertently introduce a modern touch to the surroundings. On one occasion a schoolteacher, complete with late-Victorian costume, was horrified to find her camera had begun to rewind with a loud whirring noise during a heated debate. His Lordship took matters firmly in hand, ordering the butler to 'remove the offending insect from the room at once'. The camera was whisked away to another room to die, while the actor playing his Lordship regained the focus of the debate.

The house stimulates the senses, from the smell of old books in the library to the darkness of the cellars and voices and footsteps echoing on the stairs. This is an evocative theatrical setting for both actors and students, and one which makes this extraordinary learning experience all the more memorable. ∎

LAURA HETHERINGTON

School-based drama

Some ideas from Laura Hetherington on using drama with schoolchildren.

Drama techniques can be used to create an exciting introduction to an historic house. They also offer an effective way for your pupils to relate to the building and its setting once they arrive.

The following ideas are intended for use by teachers who may not be drama specialists, but who want to introduce their children to working in role and to explore new ways of learning.

IN SCHOOL

Freeze frame

Research a particular event from the past, perhaps using a painting, and ask the children to depict that event as if the characters involved had been caught in a photograph. Facial expressions, stances and positions are all vital in conveying emotion and feelings towards other characters. The children should be invited to step in and out of the freeze-frame to comment on each other and to decide if the picture is working. When everybody is happy with the effect, it can be moved forward or backward in time. This exercise can help pupils to reflect on the motivations and feelings of figures from the past.

Director's cut

Sit your pupils in a circle and begin a scene in the centre. Ask them to enter the scene when they feel confident enough, until three or four children are improvising. Any pupil can then stop or start the drama and invite the actors to try out a different approach, by asking 'What if?'. What if she or he had said something else? What if a different decision was made there? What if there was a pause? What if one of the actors used a different tone of voice?

Facial expressions, stances and positions are all vital in conveying emotion

Object lesson

Place two or three objects or pieces of clothing in the centre of the room and, as a group, build up a picture of the person who might have owned them. Then suggest to the class that this person is missing; they have been called to the local police station because in some way, however small, they knew him or her. Each is questioned in turn to find out their connection.

ON SITE

First impressions

Before entering the house, ask the group to think of words to describe the building and the feelings it engenders. They should then use these words to decide what sort of person the house would be.

Working from objects

Divide pupils into groups of six, and select three objects in the house per group. Each group devises a scenario based around 'their' objects — something that may have happened in the house or something that occasioned those objects to be there.

Strange meeting

Ask each pupil to select a portrait and to build up a character using clues from the sitter's clothes, stance and expression. Improvise what happens when two characters from different paintings meet.

Problem-solving

Use a portrait of one of the past owners of the house to create a character. You, the teacher, then 'become' that person under the direction of your pupils. In role, tell the children that you have asked them to come to the house today to help you with a problem. This may be financial (despite your apparent wealth your outgoings exceed your income), personal (you need to find a suitable husband or wife), or domestic (the servants are insolent and disobedient).

For sale

Pupils arrive at a country house as estate agents in competition for the commission to sell the property. You can work in role as the owner, deciding who is going to obtain the best price, and introducing different conditions. Perhaps you don't wish the new owners to use the estate for certain purposes (a country club or a hotel), or perhaps certain areas are to be held back from the sale.

On the box

Pupils visit the house in role as TV researchers, looking for suitable locations for a new classic serial. Which rooms would be most suitable? They are also in search of ideas for props and costumes. However, they have been told they must work to a very tight budget, and as a result they have to make decisions about which objects will be most useful in reproducing the period atmosphere on the screen.

Jobseekers

Pupils adopt the role of young Victorian school leavers who have come to the local Big House in search of jobs as domestic servants. The teacher interviews them in role as the butler or housekeeper and takes them on a tour of the house, showing them what their duties will be. In the course of the tour, the teacher might also let it be known that for every young person who is given a job on the staff, an older servant will be dismissed and left homeless. How do the prospective employees react to this?

FOLLOW-UP ACTIVITIES AFTER A TiE PRODUCTION

Decisions, decisions

Discuss each character in terms of decisions they made. Choose a particular turning point in the action and ask the class to re-enact the play from that moment, assuming a different decision.

Hot seat

'Hot-seat' different characters to discover their feelings at various points in the performance. Either the pupils could take the part of the characters, or perhaps the teacher might do so while the class ask the questions.

Persuasion

The aim of this exercise is for pupils to find ways of persuading a character from the show to behave differently. Half the class should choose arguments for one course of action, and the other half must pick opposing arguments. Ask the children to form two lines; the character (played by the teacher) walks between the lines, listening to each side in turn.

Close of play

Pupils could think about the ending of the play. In groups, they should find ways of showing their ideal ending, and the conclusion they think would have been most likely given the historical period, the situation and the characters involved. ∎

'Hot-seating' different characters can help to discover their feelings at various points in the performance

Further reading

Arts Council of Great Britain, **Drama in Schools**, Arts Council (1991).

D. Barlow and D. Isenberg, *The use of drama in history teaching*, **Teaching History 4** (November 1970), pp 303-8.

G. Bolton, **Towards a Theory of Drama in Education**, Longman (1980).

Gavin Bolton, *Drama in education and TiE – a comparison*, in Tony Jackson (ed.), **Learning Through Theatre – New Perspectives on Theatre in Education**, Routledge (1993).

Roger Butts (ed.), **Arts in Trust – an Anthology of Writing**, Cornwall LEA (1992).

P. Coggin, **Drama and Education – an Historical Survey**, Thames & Hudson (1956).

Department of Education and Science, **Drama from 5 to 16**, Curriculum Matters 17, HMSO (1989).

J. Fairclough and P. Redsell, **Living History – Reconstructing the Past with Children**, Historic Buildings and Monuments Commission (1985).

J. Fines and R. Verrier, **The Drama of History**, New University Education (1974).

J. Fines and J. Nichol, *Domesday Book – past and present*, **Teaching History 44** (February 1986), pp 5-9.

Ken Goulding, **Art, Design and the Performing Arts**, Pluto Press (1994).

Dorothy Heathcote, **Collected Writings on Education and Drama**, Hutchinson (1984).

J. Hodgson (ed.), **The Uses of Drama – Sources Giving a Background to Acting as a Social and Educational Force**, Eyre Methuen (1972).

Tony Jackson, *Education or theatre? The development of TiE in Britain*, in Tony Jackson (ed.), **Learning Through Theatre – New Perspectives on Theatre in Education**, Routledge (1993).

K. Katner et al, **The Role of Drama in the Teaching and Learning of History**, SE Hants Drama Centre (1988).

V. Little, *What is historical imagination?*, **Teaching History 36** (June 1983), pp 27-32.

V. Little, *History through drama with top juniors*, **Teaching History II, 2** (Autumn 1983), pp 12-18.

C. Marshall, *Off with his head?*, **Junior Education** (August 1986), pp 26-7.

Honor Rhone, *Acting out the past*, **National Trust Education Supplement** (Autumn 1990), pp 1-3.

Ken Robinson, *Evaluating TiE*, in Tony Jackson (ed.), **Learning Through Theatre – New Perspectives on Theatre in Education**, Routledge (1993).

A. Tinniswood, *Re-creation, recreation or creation?*, **Resources for Education 10** (1986).

J. Tucker, *Drama and the moral dimension*, **2D – Drama and Dance** (Autumn 1985), pp 30-53.

B. Wagner, **Dorothy Heathcote – Drama as a Learning Medium**, National Education Association, Washington DC (1978).

Viv Wilson and Jayne Woodhouse, **History Through Drama – a Teachers' Guide**, Historical Association (1990).